Mindfully Grounded: A Guide To Overcoming Anxiety Through Meditation

THOMAS M RODRIGUEZ III

Copyright © 2023 Thomas M Rodriguez III

All rights reserved.

ISBN: 979-8-8616-1207-4

MINDFULLY GROUNDED: A GUIDE TO OVERCOMING ANXIETY
THROUGH MEDITATION

DEDICATION

This book is dedicated to the people trapped in the web of anxiety. May this book serve to give them the easy to implement tools to live a more enjoyable peaceful life.

MINDFULLY GROUNDED: A GUIDE TO OVERCOMING ANXIETY THROUGH MEDITATION

Leave a 1-Click Review!

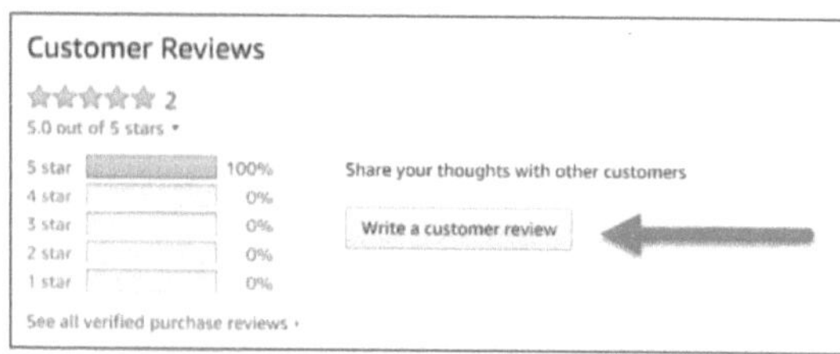

I would be incredibly thankful if you could take just 60 seconds to write a brief review on Amazon, even if it's just a few sentences!

>> Click here to leave a quick review

Other Books You'll Love

THOMAS M RODRIGUEZ III

CONTENTS

ACKNOWLEDGMENTS

To Veronica and Jake, I thank you both for being patient, understanding and encouraging during the time it took to write this book. I couldn't have done it without you.

MEDITATION

INTRODUCTION

Anxiety, a common and persistent force in our lives, can deeply impact our mental, emotional, and physical well-being. It appears as a racing heartbeat, restless thoughts, and tense feelings in our bodies. It has the ability to consume us, leaving us feeling overwhelmed and trapped in a cycle of worry and fear.

But what if there was a way to find comfort in all this chaos? What if we could achieve a state of calm and clarity amidst anxiety's grip?

THOMAS M RODRIGUEZ III

This is where mindfulness comes in.

Mindfulness, is the practice of being fully present in the moment without judgment, has gained attention as a potential solution for anxiety. By purposefully focusing on the present moment, we direct our attention away from the thoughts and worries that feed our anxiety. This simple but powerful practice holds the potential to alleviate the burden of anxiety and guide us towards inner peace.

In "Mindfully Grounded: A Guide to Overcoming Anxiety through Meditation," I share my personal journey of grappling with anxiety and discovering the transformative power of mindfulness. I vividly recall the countless sleepless nights and constant unease that plagued me. Each day felt like an uphill battle as anxiety consumed my thoughts and actions. It was during my most challenging times that I found meditation as a lifeline.

Through mindfulness meditation, I learned to observe and accept my anxious thoughts without getting caught up in them. I discovered how to cultivate stability and groundedness by anchoring myself in the present moment. Each passing day brought newfound peace and resilience that helped me navigate life's uncertainties with grace and ease.The goal of this book is to provide you with practical tools and techniques to integrate mindfulness into your daily life, enabling you to manage and reduce anxiety. From guided meditations to breathing exercises and mindfulness practices, these tools can transform your

MINDFULLY GROUNDED: A GUIDE TO OVERCOMING ANXIETY THROUGH MEDITATION

relationship with anxiety and empower you on your journey towards inner peace.

 By adopting a mindful approach, you can learn to observe your anxiety with compassion and without judgment, gradually diminishing its hold on you. This book will serve as your guide, directing you towards a grounded and serene state of being.

Join me in transformation as we explore the power of mindfulness and embark on a path of self-discovery, healing, and liberation. Let us become mindfully grounded and reclaim our lives from anxiety's grip.

Are you ready to take this journey towards inner peace? Let's begin

CHAPTER 1: UNDERSTANDING ANXIETY

Anxiety is a normal and natural emotion that humans experience from time to time. It can assist in dealing with stressful situations, such as studying for an exam, giving a presentation, or facing a challenge. However, when anxiety becomes excessive, persistent, or irrational, it can disrupt daily functioning and well-being. Anxiety can lead to feelings of nervousness, restlessness, fear, or being overwhelmed. It can also manifest in physical symptoms, including a rapid heart rate, sweating, trembling, shortness of breath, or nausea.

Anxiety disorders encompass a group of mental health conditions that go beyond temporary worry or fear. Individuals with anxiety disorders frequently experience intense, excessive, and long-lasting worry and fear regarding everyday situations. These disorders often involve recurring episodes of sudden and intense anxiety and fear, known as panic attacks, which reach their peak within minutes. Such anxiety and panic can hinder daily activities, prove challenging to control, appear disproportionate to the actual danger, and persist for extended periods. People with anxiety disorders may avoid specific places or situations to prevent the onset of these feelings[1].

Various types of anxiety disorders exist, each with its own symptoms and causes. Some of the most prevalent ones include:

Generalized anxiety disorder (GAD)

This condition entails persistent and excessive anxiety and worry regarding activities or events, even those that are ordinary or routine. The worry is disproportionate to the actual circumstances, difficult to manage, and can manifest physically. It often occurs alongside other anxiety disorders or depression[2].

Panic disorder

This disorder involves recurring and unforeseen panic attacks. Panic attacks are sudden periods of intense fear, discomfort, or a sense of losing control, even when there is no apparent danger or trigger. During a panic attack, individuals may experience symptoms such as a racing or pounding heart, sweating, trembling, chest pain, or a feeling of impending doom[2].

Social anxiety disorder

This disorder encompasses an intense and persistent fear of scrutiny and judgment by others. For individuals with social anxiety disorder, the fear of social situations can be so intense that it seems beyond their control. This fear may hinder their ability to work, attend school, or engage in everyday activities[2].

Specific phobias

These are intense fears or aversions to particular objects or situations. While anxiety in certain circumstances can be warranted, individuals with phobias experience fear that is disproportionate to the actual danger posed by the situation or object. Common specific phobias include fear of flying, fear of enclosed spaces, and fear of spiders[2].

The causes of anxiety disorders remain unknown but likely involve a combination of genetic, environmental, psychological, and developmental factors. Anxiety disorders can be hereditary, suggesting that a blend of genes and environmental stressors can contribute to their development[2]. Some potential factors contributing to anxiety disorders include:

Changes in brain chemicals and functioning

These disorders may be associated with abnormal levels of certain neurotransmitters in the brain. Neurotransmitters are chemical messengers that transmit information between nerve cells. Disruption or imbalance in the brain's circuits involving these neurotransmitters can influence how emotions and behaviors are processed[3].

Environmental stress

Stressful or traumatic life events, such as abuse, violence, divorce, the loss of a loved one, or natural disasters, can trigger or exacerbate anxiety disorders for some individuals[3]. Other sources of stress may include work pressure, school demands, family conflicts, health issues, or financial difficulties.

Family history

Individuals with relatives who have anxiety disorders are more susceptible to developing these disorders themselves. This may be due to genetic factors making certain individuals more vulnerable to anxiety or environmental factors influencing their coping mechanisms with stress[3].

Other medical conditions

Certain physical health problems may cause or contribute to anxiety disorders. For instance, heart problems, diabetes, thyroid issues, respiratory disorders, or chronic pain can produce symptoms that either mimic or worsen anxiety[3]. Anxiety may also arise as a side effect of specific medications or substances.

Substance abuse

Some individuals may turn to drugs or alcohol as a means of coping with their anxiety symptoms. However, such substances can lead to addiction and exacerbate the underlying condition[3]. Furthermore, withdrawal from drugs or alcohol can provoke or heighten anxiety.

Anxiety disorders can significantly impact daily life and overall well being. People with anxiety disorders may experience:

Mental distress

Anxiety disorders can evoke negative emotions such as fear, worry, nervousness, irritability, or anger, which affect mood and self-esteem[4]. They can also impair cognitive functions, including attention, concentration, memory, or decision-making[4].

Physical discomfort

Anxiety disorders can trigger unpleasant physical sensations like palpitations, sweating, trembling, shortness of breath, nausea, or dizziness, which can interfere with daily activities or cause distress[4]. They can also heighten the risk of developing other health problems, such as headaches, muscle tension, digestive issues, or insomnia[4].

Social impairment

Anxiety disorders can affect social relationships and functioning. Individuals with anxiety disorders may isolate themselves, avoid anxiety-inducing situations, or struggle with communication and self-expression[4]. They may also encounter difficulties at work or school, such as reduced performance, absenteeism, or conflicts with peers or authority figures[4].

Quality of life

Anxiety disorders can diminish the quality of life for those affected by them. Fears or worries can limit opportunities, choices, or goals. Individuals may also experience reduced satisfaction, happiness, or fulfillment in their personal or professional lives[4].

So in summary anxiety disorders represent a range of mental illnesses that go beyond temporary worry or fear. They have various symptoms and causes that influence different aspects of life and well-being. In the next chapter we will see how mindfulness can assist in coping with anxiety and enhancing mental and physical health.

References:

1: Anxiety disorders – Symptoms and causes – Mayo Clinic 2: NIMH » Anxiety Disorders 3: Anxiety disorder – Wikipedia 4: The Impact of Anxiety Disorders on Quality of Life and Well-Being

CHAPTER 2: INTRODUCTION TO MINDFULNESS MEDITATION

Mindful meditation is a practice that can help you cultivate inner peace by reducing stress and increasing awareness. But to reap the benefits you need to prepare yourself and your environment for it. In this chapter, we will discuss how to create an environment conducive to meditation, set intentions and goals for your meditation practice, and establish a consistent routine.

Creating a Suitable Environment for Meditation

To prepare for mindful meditation, it is important to create a suitable environment that promotes relaxation and minimizes distractions. Here are some tips to help you create that space:

Find a quiet and comfortable place

Choose a location where you can feel safe and relaxed. This could be your bedroom, living room, garden, or any other place that brings you peace.

Declutter and tidy up

A cluttered space can lead to a cluttered mind. Remove any unnecessary items from your meditation area and ensure it is clean and organized.

Set the right ambience

Adjust the lighting, temperature, and ventilation to suit your preferences. Dim the lights or light candles to create a soothing atmosphere. Use a fan, heater, or air conditioner to regulate the temperature. Open a window or use an air purifier to freshen the air.

Use props for comfort

Enhance your sitting posture and comfort by using cushions, chairs, mats, blankets, or pillows. You can also incorporate tools such as timers, music, or guided meditation apps to aid your practice.

Ensure privacy and silence

Inform your family members, roommates, or neighbors that you will be meditating and request not to be disturbed. Turn off electronic devices that may interrupt your practice.

Setting Intentions and Goals for Meditation Practice

Setting intentions and goals for your meditation practice helps you stay focused and motivated. Here are some suggestions for effectively establishing intentions and goals:

Choose a meaningful intention

Select a positive statement that aligns with your purpose for meditation. Examples include "I meditate to calm my mind" or "I meditate to cultivate compassion." Repeat your intention before, during, or after your practice.

Define realistic and measurable goals

Set specific outcomes that you want to achieve through meditation. For instance, "I want to meditate for 10 minutes every day" or "I want to reduce my anxiety level by 50%." Monitor your progress and adjust your goals accordingly.

Embrace affirmations

Use positive statements to reinforce your confidence and belief in yourself and your practice. Statements like "I am capable of

meditating" or "I am grateful for this opportunity" can enhance your mindset. Repeat your affirmations before, during, or after your meditation session.

Establishing a Consistent Meditation Routine

Consistency is key in building a meditation habit. Here are some tips to help you establish a regular meditation routine.

Choose a convenient time

Determine the most suitable time for your meditation practice based on your schedule and personal preferences. Whether it's in the morning, afternoon, evening, or night, find a time that works for you.

Gradually increase duration

Begin with shorter meditation durations, such as 5 minutes, and gradually extend the time as you become more comfortable and experienced. Adjust the duration based on your mood and energy levels.

Explore different techniques

Experiment with various meditation techniques, such as breath awareness, body scan, or loving-kindness meditation. Find a technique that resonates with you and suits your individual needs.

Reward yourself

After each meditation session, indulge in activities that bring you joy, like listening to music, reading a book, or enjoying a snack. Celebrate milestones such as completing a week or month of meditation by treating yourself to something special.

By taking the necessary steps to prepare for mindful meditation, including creating a suitable environment, setting intentions and goals, and establishing a consistent routine, you can enhance your meditation experience. These preparations will help you derive the maximum benefits and create a harmonious atmosphere for your practice. In the next chapter, we will delve into the practical aspects of mindful meditation and what you can expect from it.

CHAPTER 3: PREPARING FOR MINDFUL MEDITATION

One of the key aspects of mindfulness meditation is to develop a deeper awareness of your body and its responses to thoughts and emotions. The mind and body have a strong connection, influencing each other in various ways. For example, anxiety may cause an increased heart rate, muscle tension, or sweating. On the other hand, when you relax your body, your mind may also calm down, reducing negative thoughts.

This chapter explores how you can cultivate body awareness by scanning and observing physical sensations. The goal is to observe these sensations without judgment or the need to change them. This practice helps you become more aware of the signals your body sends and how they relate to your mental state. By paying attention to your body, you can release tension, discomfort, and cultivate a sense of ease and well-being.

A simple way to practice body awareness is through a body scan meditation. This technique involves systematically moving your attention through different parts of your body, noticing any sensations that arise. You can do this while lying down or sitting comfortably, with your eyes closed or slightly open.

To begin, take a few deep breaths and relax your shoulders. Focus your attention on your feet and toes. Feel the contact with the floor, the texture of your socks or shoes, and observe any sensations like pressure, tingling, warmth, coldness, or numbness. If thoughts or emotions arise, briefly acknowledge them and gently bring your attention back to your feet.

Move your attention to your lower legs, knees, upper legs, and continue until you reach the top of your head. Spend a few moments on each part of your body, observing the sensations without judgment. You may notice areas that are tense or relaxed, sensitive or dull, pleasant or unpleasant. Avoid labeling them as good or bad, simply observe them as they are.

During the body scan, you may become aware of areas related to anxiety, such as tightness in the chest, a knot in the stomach, or a lump in the throat. Instead of avoiding or resisting these sensations, approach them with curiosity and compassion. Breathe into them, allowing them to soften. You may find that they change or dissolve as you pay attention to them.

After scanning your entire body, take a moment to notice how you feel overall. Accept whatever you feel without trying to change it. Gently open your eyes and return to the present moment.

You can practice this body scan meditation for any duration, from a few minutes to half an hour or more. It is especially helpful when feeling stressed or anxious, as it helps relax the body and increase awareness of internal sensations.

Another technique to cultivate body awareness is progressive muscle relaxation (PMR). This involves tensing and relaxing different muscle groups in a sequential order, creating contrast and letting go of unnecessary stress.

Find a comfortable position where you can relax without disturbance, either lying down or sitting up straight. Take a few deep breaths and close your eyes if desired.

Focus on one muscle group at a time, such as your hands, arms, shoulders, neck, face, chest, abdomen, back, legs, and feet. For each group, follow these steps:

- Tense the muscles as hard as you can for about 5 seconds.
- Relax the muscles completely for about 10 seconds.
- Notice the difference between tension and relaxation in that muscle group, observing any sensations.
- Move on to the next muscle group and repeat.

After completing all muscle groups, scan your whole body and notice how you feel. You may feel more relaxed, calm, and refreshed. Physical symptoms of anxiety may also decrease or disappear.

Practice PMR for about 15 to 20 minutes, once or twice a day. You can use this technique whenever you feel tense or anxious, such as before a stressful event or during a panic attack. It helps reduce anxiety and improves your physical and mental well-being.

Deep breathing is another effective technique for cultivating body awareness and relaxation. When you breathe deeply, you send a signal to your brain that you are safe and relaxed, which in turn reduces your heart rate, blood pressure, and muscle tension.

To practice deep breathing, find a comfortable position where you can breathe freely, either lying down or sitting up straight. Place one hand on your chest and the other on your abdomen. Breathe in slowly through your nose, filling your abdomen first and then your chest. Your abdomen should rise more than your chest as you inhale. Hold your breath for a few seconds and then exhale slowly through your mouth, emptying your chest first and then your abdomen. Your abdomen should fall more than your chest as you exhale. Repeat this cycle for several minutes, maintaining smooth and even breaths.

As you practice deep breathing, focus on the sensations of the air entering and leaving your body. Observe how your abdomen and chest expand and contract. Notice the warmth and coolness of the air. Allow thoughts and emotions to come and go without attachment.

Practice deep breathing for about 10 to 15 minutes, once or twice a day. You can also use it whenever you feel anxious or overwhelmed, such as during a stressful situation or when you have difficulty sleeping. It helps relax your body and mind, allowing you to cope with anxiety more effectively.

These are just a few techniques to cultivate body awareness and encourage relaxation and release of tension. There are many other methods you can explore, such as yoga, tai chi, massage, acupuncture, and aromatherapy. Find what works best for you and make it a regular practice.

By paying attention to your body and learning to relax it, you can reduce anxiety symptoms and improve your overall health and well-being. Developing a positive and respectful relationship with your body is essential for mindfulness meditation.

In the next chapter, we will discuss how to cultivate mind awareness, observe, and manage your thoughts and emotions with mindfulness.

CHAPTER 4: MINDFUL BREATHING TECHNIQUES

Breathing is a vital function that sustains our life and health. However, breathing is also a powerful tool that can influence our mind and emotions. In this chapter, we will introduce some basic breathing exercises that can help you calm your mind and body, explain the connection between breath and emotions, and provide step-by-step instructions for various breathing techniques.

Basic Breathing Exercises for Calming the Mind and Body

One of the simplest and most effective ways to practice mindful meditation is to focus on your breath. By paying attention to your breath, you can anchor yourself in the present moment, relax your nervous system, and reduce stress and anxiety. Here are some basic breathing exercises that you can try anytime and anywhere.

Deep breathing

Deep breathing is a technique that involves inhaling deeply through your nose and exhaling slowly through your mouth. Deep breathing can help you lower your heart rate, blood pressure, and muscle tension. To practice deep breathing, follow these steps:

- Sit or lie down in a comfortable position with your spine straight and your shoulders relaxed.
- Place one hand on your chest and the other on your abdomen.
- Breathe in slowly through your nose, filling your abdomen with air. You should feel your abdomen rise as you inhale.
- Breathe out slowly through your mouth, emptying your abdomen of air. You should feel your abdomen fall as you exhale.
- Repeat this cycle for several minutes, focusing on the sensation of your breath.

Equal breathing

Equal breathing is a technique that involves inhaling and exhaling for the same duration. Equal breathing can help you balance your nervous system, calm your mind, and improve your concentration. To practice equal breathing, follow these steps:

- Sit or lie down in a comfortable position with your spine straight and your shoulders relaxed.
- in through your nose for a count of four, filling your lungs with air.
- Breathe out through your nose for a count of four, emptying your lungs of air.

Repeat this cycle for several minutes, focusing on the rhythm of your breath.

Alternate nostril breathing

Alternate nostril breathing is a technique that involves alternating the nostrils that you breathe through. Alternate nostril breathing can help you balance the left and right hemispheres of your brain, harmonize your energy, and enhance your awareness. To practice alternate nostril breathing, follow these steps:

- Sit in a comfortable position with your spine straight and your shoulders relaxed.
- Use your right thumb to close your right nostril and breathe in through your left nostril for a count of four.
- Use your right ring finger to close your left nostril and breathe out through your right nostril for a count of four.

- Breathe in through your right nostril for a count of four, keeping your left nostril closed.

- Breathe out through your left nostril for a count of four, keeping your right nostril closed.

- Repeat this cycle for several minutes, alternating the nostrils that you breathe through.

The Connection Between Breath and Emotions

Breath and emotions are closely connected. The way we breathe can affect how we feel, and the way we feel can affect how we breathe. For example, when we are anxious, we tend to breathe faster and shallower, which can increase our heart rate, blood pressure, and stress hormones. On the other hand, when we are relaxed, we tend to breathe slower and deeper, which can decrease our heart rate, blood pressure, and stress hormones.

By becoming aware of our breath and emotions, we can use our breath to regulate our emotions. For example, if we notice that we are feeling anxious, we can use deep breathing to calm ourselves down. If we notice that we are feeling depressed, we can use equal breathing to energize ourselves up. If we notice that we are feeling confused, we can use alternate nostril breathing to clear our mind.

By using our breath to regulate our emotions, we can also improve our mental health and well-being. Research has shown that mindful breathing can reduce anxiety, depression, insomnia, pain, and post-traumatic stress disorder. Mindful breathing can also enhance cognitive functions such as attention, memory, creativity, and decision making.

Step-by-Step Instructions for Various Breathing Techniques

In addition to the basic breathing exercises that we introduced earlier, there are many other breathing techniques that you can try to enhance your mindful meditation practice. Here are some examples of various breathing techniques that you can explore:

Lion's breath

Lion's breath is a technique that involves exhaling forcefully with an open mouth and tongue out. Lion's breath can help you release tension from your face, throat, and chest, as well as express your emotions and boost your confidence. To practice lion's breath, follow these steps:

- Sit or kneel in a comfortable position with your spine straight and your shoulders relaxed.
- Inhale deeply through your nose, filling your lungs with air.

- Exhale forcefully through your mouth, making a "ha" sound and sticking your tongue out as far as you can. You can also make a fierce expression with your eyes and eyebrows.

-

- Repeat this cycle several times, feeling the energy and power of your breath.

Belly Breathing

Belly breathing is a technique that involves breathing from your diaphragm, which is the muscle that separates your chest and abdomen. Belly breathing can help you breathe more efficiently, increase your oxygen intake, and improve your digestion. To practice belly breathing, follow these steps:

Lie down on your back with your knees bent and your feet flat on the floor. You can also place a pillow under your head and knees for support.

- Place one hand on your chest and the other on your belly.

- Breathe in through your nose, expanding your belly as much as you can. You should feel your belly rise as you inhale.
- Breathe out through your mouth, contracting your belly as much as you can. You should feel your belly fall as you exhale.
- Repeat this cycle for several minutes, focusing on the movement of your belly.

4-7-8 Breathing

4-7-8 breathing is a technique that involves inhaling for four seconds, holding for seven seconds, and exhaling for eight seconds. 4-7-8 breathing can help you relax your nervous system, calm your mind, and induce sleep. To practice 4-7-8 breathing, follow these steps:

- Sit or lie down in a comfortable position with your spine straight and your shoulders relaxed.
- Breathe in through your nose for a count of four, filling your lungs with air.
- Hold your breath for a count of seven, keeping your lungs full of air.
  Breathe out through your mouth for a count of eight, emptying your lungs of air. You can also make a gentle "whoosh" sound as you exhale.

- Repeat this cycle four times, or until you feel relaxed.

In this chapter, we discussed some mindful breathing techniques that can help you overcome anxiety through meditation. We introduced

29

some basic breathing exercises for calming the mind and body, explained the connection between breath and emotions, and provided step-by-step instructions for various breathing techniques. By practicing these techniques regularly, you can enhance your mindful meditation experience and enjoy the benefits of mindful breathing. In the next chapter, we will explore how to practice mindful meditation in different situations and contexts.

CHAPTER 5: CULTIVATING BODY AWARENESS

One of the key aspects of mindfulness meditation is to develop a deeper awareness of your body and its responses to thoughts and emotions. The mind and body have a strong connection, influencing each other in various ways. For example, anxiety may cause an increased heart rate, muscle tension, or sweating. On the other hand, when you relax your body, your mind may also calm down, reducing negative thoughts.

This chapter explores how you can cultivate body awareness by scanning and observing physical sensations. The goal is to observe these sensations without judgment or the need to change them. This practice helps you become more aware of the signals your body sends and how they relate to your mental state. By paying attention to your body, you can release tension, discomfort, and cultivate a sense of ease and well-being.

A simple way to practice body awareness is through a body scan meditation. This technique involves systematically moving your attention through different parts of your body, noticing any sensations that arise. You can do this while lying down or sitting comfortably, with your eyes closed or slightly open.

To begin, take a few deep breaths and relax your shoulders. Focus your attention on your feet and toes. Feel the contact with the floor, the texture of your socks or shoes, and observe any sensations like pressure, tingling, warmth, coldness, or numbness. If thoughts or emotions arise, briefly acknowledge them and gently bring your attention back to your feet.

Move your attention to your lower legs, knees, upper legs, and continue until you reach the top of your head. Spend a few moments on each part of your body, observing the sensations without judgment. You may notice areas that are tense or relaxed,

sensitive or dull, pleasant or unpleasant. Avoid labeling them as good or bad, simply observe them as they are.

During the body scan, you may become aware of areas related to anxiety, such as tightness in the chest, a knot in the stomach, or a lump in the throat. Instead of avoiding or resisting these sensations, approach them with curiosity and compassion. Breathe into them, allowing them to soften. You may find that they change or dissolve as you pay attention to them.

After scanning your entire body, take a moment to notice how you feel overall. Accept whatever you feel without trying to change it. Gently open your eyes and return to the present moment.

You can practice this body scan meditation for any duration, from a few minutes to half an hour or more. It is especially helpful when feeling stressed or anxious, as it helps relax the body and increase awareness of internal sensations.

Another technique to cultivate body awareness is progressive muscle relaxation (PMR). This involves tensing and relaxing different muscle groups in a sequential order, creating contrast and letting go of unnecessary stress.

Find a comfortable position where you can relax without disturbance, either lying down or sitting up straight. Take a few deep breaths and close your eyes if desired.

Focus on one muscle group at a time, such as your hands, arms, shoulders, neck, face, chest, abdomen, back, legs, and feet. For each group, follow these steps:

- Tense the muscles as hard as you can for about 5 seconds.
- Relax the muscles completely for about 10 seconds.
- Notice the difference between tension and relaxation in that muscle group, observing any sensations.
- Move on to the next muscle group and repeat.

After completing all muscle groups, scan your whole body and notice how you feel. You may feel more relaxed, calm, and refreshed. Physical symptoms of anxiety may also decrease or disappear.

Practice PMR for about 15 to 20 minutes, once or twice a day. You can use this technique whenever you feel tense or anxious, such as before a stressful event or during a panic attack. It helps reduce anxiety and improves your physical and mental well-being.

Deep breathing is another effective technique for cultivating body awareness and relaxation. When you breathe deeply, you send a signal to your brain that you are safe and relaxed, which in turn reduces your heart rate, blood pressure, and muscle tension.

To practice deep breathing, find a comfortable position where you can breathe freely, either lying down or sitting up straight. Place one hand on your chest and the other on your abdomen. Breathe in

slowly through your nose, filling your abdomen first and then your chest. Your abdomen should rise more than your chest as you inhale.

Hold your breath for a few seconds and then exhale slowly through your mouth, emptying your chest first and then your abdomen. Your abdomen should fall more than your chest as you exhale. Repeat this cycle for several minutes, maintaining smooth and even breaths.

As you practice deep breathing, focus on the sensations of the air entering and leaving your body. Observe how your abdomen and chest expand and contract. Notice the warmth and coolness of the air. Allow thoughts and emotions to come and go without attachment.

Practice deep breathing for about 10 to 15 minutes, once or twice a day. You can also use it whenever you feel anxious or overwhelmed, such as during a stressful situation or when you have difficulty sleeping. It helps relax your body and mind, allowing you to cope with anxiety more effectively.

These are just a few techniques to cultivate body awareness and encourage relaxation and release of tension. There are many other methods you can explore, such as yoga, tai chi, massage, acupuncture, and aromatherapy. Find what works best for you and make it a regular practice.

By paying attention to your body and learning to relax it, you can reduce anxiety symptoms and improve your overall health and well-being. Developing a positive and respectful relationship with your body is essential for mindfulness meditation.

In the next chapter, we will discuss how to cultivate mind awareness, observe, and manage your thoughts and emotions with mindfulness.

CHAPTER 6: OBSERVING THOUGHTS AND EMOTIONS

In this chapter, we will explore practices that can help you observe and detach from your thoughts and emotions, allowing you to have a more balanced and objective perspective on them. By cultivating mindfulness, you can reduce the impact of negative thoughts and emotions on your anxiety.

Practice 1: Mindful Breathing

Mindful breathing is a powerful technique that helps calm the mind and body while creating distance from your thoughts and emotions.

Find a comfortable position, close your eyes or lower your gaze, and bring your attention to your breath. Notice how it feels as it enters and leaves your body, without trying to change or control it. If your mind wanders, gently bring it back to your breath, without judgment or frustration. Continue this practice for as long as you like or until you feel more centered and calm.

Practice 2: Mindful Observation

Mindful observation involves choosing an object in your environment and focusing your attention on it with curiosity and openness. Notice its shape, color, texture, and other details. Compare it to other objects and appreciate its uniqueness. If thoughts or emotions arise, simply observe them without attachment and return your attention to the object. Practice mindful observation for as long as you like or until you feel more present and aware.

.

Practice 3: Mindful Labeling

Mindful labeling helps you identify and name your thoughts and emotions without judgment or reaction. Find a quiet place and become aware of your inner experience. Label each thought or emotion with a word or phrase that accurately describes it. Avoid analyzing, evaluating, or changing them; simply acknowledge and name them. If you notice any physical sensations, label them as well. Practice mindful labeling for as long as you like or until you feel more calm and clear.

PThese practices can be integrated into your daily routine to cultivate mindfulness and develop the ability to observe and detach from your thoughts and emotions. By doing so, you can reduce the impact of anxiety triggers and gain a greater sense of control over your mental and emotional well-being.

In the next chapter, we will explore strategies for responding to anxiety-provoking situations with mindfulness and compassion.

CHAPTER 7: CULTIVATING COMPASSION AND SELF CARE

Anxiety can often lead to feelings of isolation, insecurity, and self-doubt. It can also cause us to be overly critical and harsh towards ourselves and others. However, these negative attitudes and behaviors only serve to exacerbate our anxiety and diminish our self-esteem. They can also hinder the development of healthy relationships with ourselves and others. That's why it's crucial to prioritize compassion and self-care when managing anxiety.

Compassion involves showing empathy and kindness towards ourselves and others, especially during times of suffering or struggle. Self-care, on the other hand, entails taking proactive steps to improve our mental health and overall well-being. Both compassion and self-care can help us navigate anxiety in a more positive and constructive manner. They can also enhance our happiness, resilience, and sense of purpose.

In this chapter, we will explore the significance of self-compassion in managing anxiety and provide guidance on how to cultivate it through various exercises. We will also discuss self-care practices that promote mental health and well-being.

It's important for me to stress that self-compassion is not a sign of weakness or selfishness. It's in fact just the opposite, it reflects strength and wisdom. Self-compassion means acknowledging our shared humanity, understanding that making mistakes and facing challenges are part of being human. We should show ourselves the same kindness, empathy, and support we would offer to a loved one in distress.

Self-compassion can positively impact anxiety management in several ways. For instance, it can:

Diminish the intensity and frequency of negative emotions like fear, anger, shame, guilt, or sadness.

Cultivate more positive emotions such as joy, gratitude, hope, or satisfaction.

Enhance self-esteem, self-confidence, and self-acceptance.

Reduce tendencies to ruminate, worry, or avoid.

Strengthen coping skills, problem-solving abilities, and motivation.

Foster healthier relationships by increasing empathy, trust, and cooperation.

Therefore, self-compassion not only benefits ourselves but also has a ripple effect on others. By practicing compassion towards ourselves, we can extend that same compassion to others who may be facing similar or different difficulties. In doing so, we not only inspire others to be more compassionate towards themselves and us but also create a more compassionate and understanding world.

Exercise 1: Self compassion through writing

This exercise invites you to write a letter to yourself about something that causes you to feel shame, insecurity, or inadequacy from a perspective of acceptance and compassion. It helps you to express your feelings, understand your needs, and offer yourself support.

Exercise 2: self compassion through self touch

This exercise teaches you how to activate your parasympathetic nervous system by using supportive touch to help you feel calm, cared for, and safe. It involves placing your hand over your heart or

another soothing place on your body and feeling the warmth, pressure, and gentle movement of your hand.

Exercise 3: Self-Compassion Break

To me the most powerful exercise is the self-compassion break. It is a brief practice that can be done whenever you experience anxiety or stress. It involves acknowledging your emotions, reminding yourself that you are not alone, and offering yourself soothing words or gestures. To practice the self-compassion break, follow these steps:

- Find a quiet and comfortable space where you can sit or lie down without interruption.
- Close your eyes or lower your gaze and take a few deep breaths to relax.
- Bring to mind a situation that is causing you anxiety or distress. It can be something from the past, present, or even a hypothetical future event.
- Observe how your mind and body feel in response to this situation. Allow yourself to notice these feelings without judgment or resistance.

- Say to yourself: "This is a moment of suffering." You can also use other words that resonate with you, such as "This is challenging," "This is difficult," or "This is stressful."

- Remind yourself: "Suffering is part of life." Other words that can convey the same message include "Everyone experiences

-

- this," "I'm not alone in this," or "This is a common human experience."
- Direct compassion towards yourself by saying: "May I be kind to myself." You can also use alternative phrases that express your desire for self-compassion, such as "May I be gentle with myself," "May I offer myself understanding," or "May I treat myself with care."
- Place your hand over your heart or any part of your body that feels comforting. Feel the warmth and connection between your hand and your body. Take deep breaths, focusing on your heart center.
- Repeat these phrases as many times as necessary until you feel a sense of calm and compassion towards yourself.

By regularly practicing the self-compassion break, you can cultivate a more compassionate and understanding attitude towards yourself, which in turn can help alleviate anxiety and promote well-being.

Remember, cultivating self-compassion takes time and practice. Be patient with yourself throughout this journey, and remember that you deserve the same compassion and care you extend to others.

Sources:

8 Powerful Self-Compassion Exercises & Worksheets (+ PDF). https://positivepsychology.com/self-compassion-exercises-worksheet

(2) Exercises – Self-Compassion. https://self-compassion.org/category/exercises/.

(3) 8 Powerful Self-Compassion Exercises & Worksheets (+ PDF). https://positivepsychology.com/self-compassion-exercises-worksheet https://positivepsychology.com/self-compassion-exercises-worksheets/.

(4) Exercises – Self-Compassion. https://self-compassion.org/category/exercises/.

(5) Self-Compassion Exercises | Stress & Development Lab – Harvard University. https://sdlab.fas.harvard.edu/self-compassion/self-compassion-exercises/

(6) 8 Powerful Self-Compassion Exercises & Worksheets (+ PDF). https://positivepsychology.com/self-compassion-exercises-worksheet https://positivepsychology.com/self-compassion-exercises-worksheets/

(7) Self-Compassion Exercises | Stress & Development Lab – Harvard University. https://sdlab.fas.harvard.edu/self-compassion/self-compassion-exercisesses.

(8) 8 Powerful Self-Compassion Exercises & Worksheets (+ PDF). https://positivepsychology.com/self-compassion-exercises-worksheets/

(9) Exercises – Self-Compassion. https://self-compassion.org/category/exercises/.

(10) 4 Techniques for Practicing Self-Compassion – Cleveland
Clinic. https://health.clevelandclinic.org/self-compassion/.

(11) undefined.
https://self-compassion.org/exercise-2-self-compassion-break/.

(12) undefined. https://self-compassion.org/exercise-3-exploring-
self-compassion-wr https://self-compassion.org/exercise-3-
exploring-self-compassion-writing/

(13) undefined.
https://self-compassion.org/exercise-4-supportive-touch/.

CHAPTER 8: MINDFUL MOVEMENT AND EXERCISE

Anxiety can have both mental and physical effects on your body. Physical symptoms like muscle tension, rapid heartbeat, sweating, and shortness of breath can exacerbate stress and create a cycle of

anxiety. To break this cycle, you can incorporate mindful movement and exercise into your anxiety management routine. Mindful movement and exercise involve engaging in physical

activities with awareness and intention, paying attention to your body sensations, breath, and emotions. This approach allows you to benefit from both mindfulness and exercise, including:

Reducing stress hormones and increasing endorphins, which act as natural painkillers and mood boosters.

Enhancing blood circulation and oxygen delivery to your brain and body, thereby improving cognitive function and energy levels.

Releasing muscle tension and improving posture, flexibility, and balance.

Boosting self-confidence and self-esteem by providing a sense of capability and accomplishment.

Providing a healthy outlet for emotions, allowing for constructive expression and release.

There are various mindful movement practices to choose from based on your preferences and abilities. Some examples include:

Yoga

Yoga combines physical poses, breathing techniques, and meditation to calm the mind, relax the body, and foster self-connection. It also enhances strength, flexibility, and coordination. You can practice yoga at home or join a studio or online class, exploring different styles such as hatha, vinyasa, or bikram, to find what suits you best.

Walking meditation

This practice involves slow and mindful walking, paying attention to each step and breath. It helps ground you in the present moment, reduce stress, and improve concentration. You can practice walking meditation anywhere, alone or with others, in silence or with music or guided instructions.

Tai chi

Tai chi comprises graceful and fluid movements combined with coordinated breathing. It helps balance energy, calm the mind, and strengthen the body. You can practice tai chi at home or join a class at a park or community center, choosing a form such as yang or chen that matches your skill level.

To mindfully integrate physical activity into your daily routines, consider the following tips:

- Set realistic goals for frequency and duration, starting small and gradually increasing.
- Choose activities you enjoy and that fit your lifestyle, experimenting until you find the right fit.
- Schedule specific exercise times and treat them as important appointments with yourself.
- Prepare ahead of time, gathering necessary items like clothes, shoes, equipment, or a playlist to minimize procrastination.
- Prior to starting, check in with yourself, noting physical and emotional states. Set an intention for the session, focusing on what you want to achieve.

- During exercise, pay attention to body sensations, breath, and emotions. Observe how they change as you move. Adjust pace or intensity if you experience pain or discomfort. If thoughts or worries arise, gently bring your attention back to the present moment.

- After finishing, cool down and stretch. Appreciate yourself for completing the session and reflect on how you feel compared to before. Take note of any personal discoveries or lessons.

Regular practice of mindful movement and exercise can improve both physical and mental health, enhancing overall well-being. It also fosters a positive relationship with your body based on respect and gratitude.

Here are some exercises to get you started in applying what you learned in this chapter.

Choose one mindful movement practice that interests you and engage in it for at least 10 minutes. Observe how it affects your body sensations, breath, emotions, and thoughts.

Write down three benefits of mindful movement and exercise that are relevant to you. Consider how they can help you cope with anxiety.

Create a plan for mindfully integrating physical activity into your daily routines. Include the following details:

What activity will you do? Choose a specific mindful movement practice or exercise that aligns with your interests and abilities.

When will you do it? Determine the best time of day that works for you and fits into your schedule. Consider whether you prefer mornings, afternoons, or evenings.

Where will you do it? Decide whether you will practice at home, outdoors, or in a gym or studio. Consider the environment that makes you feel most comfortable and motivated.

How will you prepare for it? Plan the necessary preparations, such as gathering any equipment, setting up a dedicated space, or selecting appropriate clothing.

How will you monitor your progress? Establish a system to track your progress, whether it's through a journal, a fitness app, or simply noting your achievements and improvements.

By creating a clear plan and sticking to it, you increase the likelihood of incorporating mindful movement and exercise into your daily routines effectively. Remember to be flexible and adjust your plan as needed to accommodate any changes or new insights that arise along the way.

Remember, the goal is to approach mindful movement and exercise as an opportunity to cultivate self-awareness, reduce anxiety, and enhance your overall well-being. Enjoy the process, be kind to yourself, and celebrate your progress along the journey.

CHAPTER 9: MINDFULNESS IN DAILY LIFE

Mindfulness is not only a practice that you do in a formal setting, such as sitting on a cushion or attending a class. It is also a way of living that you can bring to every moment of your day. Mindfulness in daily life means being aware of what you are doing, feeling, and thinking, as well as how you relate to yourself and others.

By incorporating mindfulness into everyday activities, you can enjoy the following benefits:

- Enhancing your attention and focus, as you avoid distractions and multitasking
- Improving your productivity and efficiency, as you complete tasks with more clarity and quality
- Increasing your satisfaction and joy, as you appreciate the simple pleasures and beauty of life
- Reducing your stress and anxiety, as you cope with challenges and difficulties more calmly and wisely
- Developing your compassion and empathy, as you understand and respect the perspectives and feelings of others

There are many ways to bring mindful awareness to daily tasks and interactions. Here are some practical tips for maintaining mindfulness amid the busyness of life:

- Start your day with a mindful intention. Before you get out of bed, take a few moments to set an intention for your day. What do you want to achieve? How do you want to feel? How do you want to treat yourself and others? This will help you align your actions with your values and goals.
- Use reminders and cues. You can use objects, sounds, or events as reminders to be mindful throughout the day. For example, you can use your phone alarm, a bracelet, or a sticker as cues to pause and check in with yourself. You can also use transitions, such as changing rooms, starting or ending a meeting, or getting in or out of a car, as opportunities to reconnect with the present moment.

-

- Practice mindful breathing. Breathing is something that you do all the time, but often unconsciously. By paying attention to your breath, you can anchor yourself in the present moment and calm your mind and body. You can practice mindful breathing anytime, anywhere, by simply noticing the sensations of your inhalation and exhalation. You can also use a mantra or a phrase to accompany your breath, such as "I breathe in peace, I breathe out stress".

- Do one thing at a time. Multitasking may seem like an efficient way to get things done, but it actually reduces your performance and increases your stress. By doing one thing at a time, you can focus better, make fewer mistakes, and enjoy the process more. You can also apply mindfulness to whatever you are doing, by paying attention to the details and sensations of the activity. For example, if you are eating, notice the colors, textures, flavors, and aromas of the food. If you are washing dishes, notice the temperature, pressure, and movement of the water.

- Be mindful of your emotions. Emotions are natural and inevitable parts of life, but they can also affect your mood, behavior, and decisions. By being mindful of your emotions, you can acknowledge them without judging them or being overwhelmed by them. You can also express them in healthy ways that do not harm yourself or others.

- You can practice mindfulness of emotions by naming them (e.g., "I feel angry"), observing them (e.g., "Where do I feel

it in my body?"), and accepting them (e.g., "It's okay to feel
this way").

- Be mindful of your thoughts. Thoughts are also natural and
  inevitable parts of life, but they can also influence your
  perception, attitude, and actions. By being mindful of your
  thoughts, you can recognize them without believing them or
  being controlled by them. You can also challenge them if
  they are negative or irrational, and replace them with positive
  or realistic ones. You can practice mindfulness of thoughts by
  labeling them (e.g., "This is a thought"), examining them
  (e.g., "Is this true?"), and letting them go (e.g., "I don't need
  this thought").

- Be mindful of your communication. Communication is
  essential for building and maintaining relationships with
  others, but it can also be a source of conflict or
  misunderstanding. By being mindful of your communication,
  you can listen actively, speak respectfully, and respond
  appropriately. You can also avoid unnecessary arguments or
  hurtful words that may damage your relationships. You can
  practice mindfulness of communication by paying attention
  to the verbal and non-verbal cues of yourself and others (e.g.,
  tone of voice, body language), using "I" statements instead of
  "you" statements (e.g., "I feel hurt" instead of "You hurt
  me"), and asking for feedback or clarification if needed (e.g.,
  "Did I understand you correctly?").

By practicing mindfulness in daily life regularly, you can enhance
your well-being and happiness, as well as your relationships with
yourself and others. You can also cultivate a more positive and
meaningful life experience.

To help you apply what you learned in this chapter, here are some exercises that you can try.

Choose one everyday activity that you usually do mindlessly and try to do it mindfully. Pay attention to how it affects your senses, emotions, and thoughts.

Write down three benefits of mindfulness in daily life that are relevant to you. How can they help you cope with anxiety?

Create a plan for incorporating mindfulness into your daily routines. Include the following details: what activity will you do mindfully? When will you do it? Where will you do it? How will you remind yourself to do it? How will you monitor your progress?

CHAPTER 10: OVERCOMING OBSTACLES AND MAINTAINING PROGRESS

Meditation is a powerful practice that can help you overcome anxiety and live a more mindful and fulfilling life. However, meditation is not always easy or pleasant. You may encounter various obstacles along the way, such as resistance, restlessness, or lack of motivation. These obstacles can make you feel frustrated, discouraged, or tempted to give up. In this chapter, we will address some of the common challenges faced by meditators and offer some strategies for overcoming them. We will also provide some insights on how to maintain your progress and integrate mindfulness into your everyday life.

Resistance is the feeling of not wanting to meditate or avoiding it altogether. These feelings can arise for many reasons, such as fear, boredom, doubt, or discomfort. Resistance can manifest as procrastination, distraction, or rationalization. For example, you may find yourself saying things like "I don't have time to meditate today", "I'm too tired to meditate", or "Meditation doesn't work for me".

Resistance is a normal and natural reaction. It is a sign that you are facing something that challenges you or pushes you out of your comfort zone. It is also an opportunity to learn more about yourself and your patterns of thinking and behaving. Instead of judging yourself or giving in to resistance, you can use it as a catalyst for growth and transformation.

Here are some ways to overcome resistance:

Acknowledge it. The first step is to recognize and accept that you are feeling resistant. Don't try to deny or suppress it. Simply observe it with curiosity and compassion.

Investigate it. The next step is to explore the source and nature of your resistance. Ask yourself questions like "What am I afraid of?", "What am I avoiding?", "What am I believing?", or "What am I feeling?". Try to be honest and open with yourself. You may discover some underlying beliefs or emotions that are holding you back.

Challenge it. The final step is to challenge your resistance by questioning its validity and usefulness. Ask yourself questions like "Is this true?", "Is this helpful?", "Is this serving me?", or "What would happen if I did the opposite?". You may realize that your resistance is based on false assumptions or irrational fears. You may also find some positive consequences or benefits of overcoming your resistance.

Act on it. Once you have challenged your resistance, you can take action by doing what you are resisting. Even if you don't feel like it, commit to meditating for a few minutes. You may find that once you start, it becomes easier and more enjoyable than you expected. You may also feel a sense of accomplishment and empowerment after overcoming your resistance

Restlessness is the feeling of being unable to sit still or focus during meditation. Restlessness can arise from physical, mental, or emotional causes, such as fatigue, stress, boredom, excitement, or anxiety. Restlessness can manifest as fidgeting, shifting, itching, yawning, or wandering thoughts. For example, you may find yourself thinking about your plans for the day, your problems at work, or your favorite TV show.

Restlessness is normal and natural. It is a sign that you are experiencing some energy or movement in your body or mind. This is also an opportunity to practice mindfulness and concentration. Instead of judging yourself or fighting against restlessness, you can use it as a focus for your attention and awareness.

Here are some ways to overcome restlessness:

Breathe deeply. The first step is to take a few deep breaths and relax your body and mind. Breathing deeply can help you calm down and release tension. Breathing deeply can also help you anchor your attention in the present moment and create some space between you and your thoughts.

Scan your body. The next step is to scan your body from head to toe and notice any sensations that arise. You may feel warmth, coldness, tingling, tightness, heaviness, lightness, pain, pleasure, or nothing at all. Whatever you feel, just observe it with curiosity and compassion.

Label your thoughts. The final step is to label your thoughts as they come and go in your mind. You don't have to analyze or engage with them. Just name them briefly and let them pass by. For example, you may say "planning", "worrying", "remembering", "fantasizing", or "judging". Labeling your thoughts can help you detach from them and see them as mental events rather than facts.

Lack of motivation is the feeling of having no interest or enthusiasm for meditation. These feelings can arise from various factors, such as boredom, doubt, impatience, frustration, or disappointment. Lack of motivation can manifest as skipping sessions, shortening sessions, or losing focus during sessions. For example, you may find yourself saying things like "I don't see any results", "I don't enjoy this", or "I don't need this".

It is normal and natural to feel a lack of motivation. This is simply a sign that you are experiencing some challenges or changes in your meditation practice. It is also an opportunity to reevaluate and renew your commitment and intention. Instead of judging yourself or giving up on meditation, you can use it as a motivation for improvement and inspiration

Here are some ways to overcome lack of motivation:

Remind yourself of your goals. The first step is to remind yourself of why you started meditating and what you hope to achieve from it. You may have some specific goals, such as reducing anxiety, improving health, enhancing performance, or developing wisdom. You may also have some general goals, such as being happier, calmer, or more compassionate. Whatever your goals are, write them down and review them regularly.

Track your progress. The next step is to track your progress and celebrate your achievements. You can use a journal, a calendar, an app, or any other tool to record your meditation sessions and note any changes or benefits you notice. You can also use some metrics, such as the duration, frequency, quality, or satisfaction of your sessions. Tracking your progress can help you see how far you have come and how much you have learned.

Seek support. The final step is to seek support and guidance from others who share your interest and passion for meditation. You can join a meditation group, class, course, retreat, or online community. You can also find a meditation teacher, mentor, friend, or partner. Seeking support can help you learn from others' experiences and perspectives, receive feedback and encouragement, and feel connected and inspired.

Meditation is not a one-time event or a quick fix. It is a lifelong journey and a way of living. To maintain your progress and reap the benefits of meditation, you need to practice regularly and consistently. You also need to integrate mindfulness into your everyday life and apply it to various situations and challenges.

Here are some tips for maintaining progress and integrating mindfulness:

Make it a habit. The best way to ensure that you meditate regularly is to make it a habit. A habit is something that you do automatically and effortlessly without thinking about it. To form a habit, you need to choose a specific time, place, and duration for your meditation sessions and stick to them as much as possible. You also need to

create some cues and rewards that trigger and reinforce your behavior. For example, you may meditate every morning after brushing your teeth (cue) and enjoy a cup of tea afterwards (reward).

Be flexible. While having a routine and a structure can help you establish a habit, being flexible and adaptable can help you sustain it. Sometimes, life may get in the way of your plans and prevent you from meditating as usual. Instead of feeling guilty or stressed about it, you can adjust your schedule or modify your practice accordingly. For example, if you are traveling or busy, you may meditate at a different time or for a shorter duration. If you are sick or injured, you may meditate lying down or using a different technique.

Be mindful throughout the day. Meditation is not only something that you do on the cushion or the chair. It is something that you can do anytime and anywhere in your daily life. You can be mindful of whatever you are doing, such as eating, walking, working, or talking. You can also be mindful of whatever you are experiencing, such as thoughts, feelings, sensations, or sounds. Being mindful throughout the day can help you deepen your awareness, enhance your concentration, reduce your stress, and improve your well-being.

Meditation is a simple yet profound practice that can help you overcome anxiety and live a more mindful and fulfilling life. However, meditation is not always easy or pleasant. You may encounter various obstacles along the way that challenge your practice and test your patience. By applying the strategies discussed in this chapter, you can overcome these obstacles and maintain your

progress. You can also integrate mindfulness into your everyday life and apply it to various situations and challenges.

I hope that this book has been helpful and inspiring for you on your path to overcoming anxiety through meditation. I strongly encourage you to continue practicing meditation regularly and consistently. I also suggest that you explore other resources and opportunities that can support and enrich your practice.

Thank you for reading this book and sharing this journey with me. I wish you all the best in your future endeavors.

Here are some additional resources, suggested readings, and references for further exploration,

[Mindful.org]: A website that offers articles, podcasts, videos, courses, events, and more on mindfulness and meditation.

[Headspace]: An app that guides you through various meditation programs tailored to your needs and goals.

[Calm]: An app that provides relaxing music, sounds, stories, and meditations to help you sleep better and reduce stress.

[The Mindful Way through Anxiety: Break Free from Chronic Worry and Reclaim Your Life]: A book by Susan M. Orsillo and Lizabeth Roemer that teaches you how to use mindfulness-based cognitive therapy (MBCT) to overcome anxiety.

[The Anxiety Solution: A Quieter Mind, a Calmer You]: A book by Chloe Brotheridge that offers practical advice and exercises to help you cope with anxiety.

[Mindfulness: An Eight-Week Plan for Finding Peace in a Frantic World]: A book by Mark Williams and Danny Penman that introduces you to the eight-week MBCT program that has been proven to reduce stress and improve well-being.

[Wherever You Go, There You Are: Mindfulness Meditation in Everyday Life]: A book by Jon Kabat-Zinn that explains the essence and benefits of mindfulness meditation and how to apply it to various aspects of your life.

Namaste □

ABOUT THE AUTHOR

Thomas has been a Buddhist practitioner for the past 26 years. He is a master of meditation and lives in Texas with his beloved dog Jake. Thomas enjoys running for health which he does mindfully. He is the author of ,"Mindfully Grounded: A Guide To Overcoming Anxiety Through Meditation" and "Paws Of Love: Navigating Pet Loss and The Path To Healing".

Other Books You'll Love

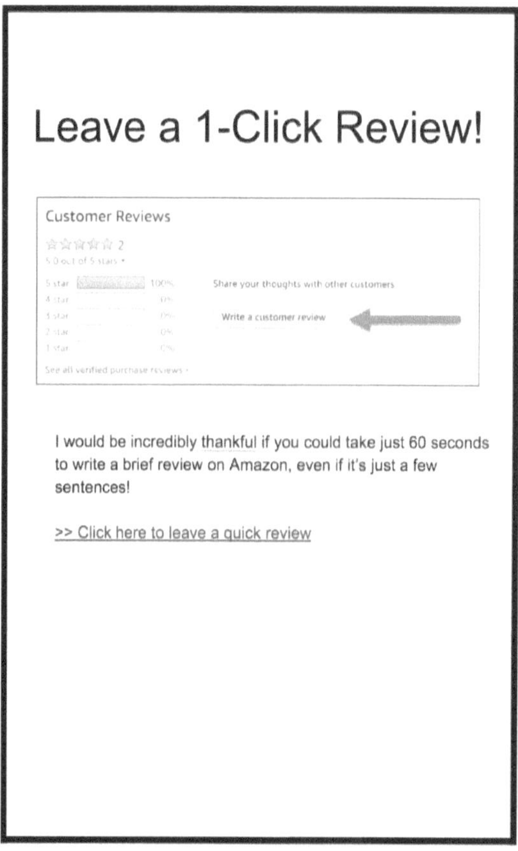

I would be incredibly thankful if you could take just 60 seconds
to write a brief review on Amazon, even if it's just a few
sentences!

>> Click here to leave a quick review

www.ingramcontent.com/pod-product-compliance
Lightning Source LLC
Chambersburg PA
CBHW031323250726
48656CB00005B/1940